WORTH DYING FOR

by Jon Coats

WORTH DYING FOR
ISBN: 978-1-936314-87-4

Produced and Distributed by
Youth Pastor In A Box, Inc
www.youthpastorinabox.com
Printed in the United States of America.

PART ONE:

FINDING WORTH

It was April 26th of 1991, while my brother and I were out playing in the yard, when it all started. The clouds grew darker and the rain began. The rain was so disappointing—we were to have baseball practice and then go right to our school's Friday Fun Night with inflatables and all sorts of games. It wasn't long after the rain began that the winds and hail followed.

My brother and I went inside to escape. Thunderstorm and tornado warnings flashed across the bottom of the television, and meteorologists talking about the storms were constantly interrupting our favorite afternoon programs. This wasn't anything new. After all, we lived in Kansas! It seemed to be the norm.

Maybe that's why I wasn't too scared at first.

Not too long after the storm started to really get serious, my mom got home. She was going to make dinner, and since baseball practice was cancelled, we would be going straight to our school's Friday Fun Night. However, the hail really began to come down and the wind starting picking up. The television screen went to static, while a reporter's voice exclaimed, "There is a tornado in South Wichita heading east!"

I was just in the third grade, so the only directions I knew were up and down. However, my mom looked at my sister, who is four years older than I am, and asked, "Which way did she say the tornado was heading?" My mom then went and opened the front door and asked my sister, "Lish, what is that?"

Being curious myself, I went to the front door to see what "that" was. "That" happened to be one of the largest tornadoes in Kansas' history. Some say it stretched to close to a mile wide at different times—and it was headed right for our mobile home. Two cameramen were filming the tornado and started telling us to run for cover. We didn't have time to do so and ran back to the back bedroom and began to pray.

After the rumbling stopped and the noises subsided, we went out our back bedroom door to what should have been the kitchen and living room—but now we could see across the street. The tornado had cut our mobile home in half! Broken water lines gushed, people screamed, and I could see mobile homes that had been flipped upside down. The two double-wides next to us were completely flattened and destroyed.

We didn't know if anyone had been killed or seriously injured, but I can remember that my thirdgrade mind could only think of one thing and one thing only—my baseball cards!

My collection of baseball cards was one to be coveted. I got to be in the "Cool Kids Club" because of my collection. I spent nearly every night organizing and looking up the prices of my baseball cards. I had at least $300 in my collection.

And now, they were all flying around in the air from the winds that had just blown through. Lives were in danger, and our home was utterly destroyed—it's amazing to think that all I cared about were my $300 worth of baseball cards.

WHO DETERMINES YOUR WORTH?

Too often in all of our lives we base what we are worth on what others think and not on what the things that really matter. For instance, we usually pick the clothes we wear, the phone we carry, and even the people we hang with because these things make us feel like we're worth more. If you don't understand, try wearing your parents' clothes to school or carrying your grandmother's ancient flip phone. While some people shop at the thrift store to get this look, for most people when we don't look cool or feel like we are, we start thinking we are worth less. All of us enjoy certain styles and different things. The problem comes when we base our worth on those things.

As a youth pastor I once sat down with a kid in our youth group. He was on the basketball team, shopped at the right stores in the mall, and had one of the most incredible jobs ever. This guy was a gamer. Not just any gamer—he was paid to travel to tournaments around the country and compete. You would think he thought he was on top of the world. However, he sat in my car and told me how depressed he was. He explained to me that the reason behind his depression was that he hadn't had a girlfriend for more than six months.

As crazy as it sounds, many of us have allowed what people think about us to determine our worth. We allow guys and girls at school, parents, coaches, teachers, and even our bosses' opinions to determine our worth. If "they" don't like us, we must be worth nothing. Our attitudes, grades, and even our lives begin to spiral downward as we continue to try our hardest to please these people—and they continue to reject us. The truth is, though these people are very important to us, they cannot determine our worth. In fact, I have found that humans are horrible at determining worth. I cared more for my $300 baseball collection than my home, my family's car, and our neighbors' lives. And we don't get any better after the third grade. People are horrible at determining worth.

For the last several years, the United States and most of the rest of the world have struggled financially. People are losing their jobs, houses, and even their families due to the financial pressures. I recently met a guy who had multiple degrees, had worked for a prestigious company and made lots of money, and when the economy tanked, he lost almost everything.

However, while the economy was falling to pieces, something very interesting happened to teen spending. It went up. Research shows that while their parents were losing houses and jobs, American teenagers ages 12-18 spent over 40 billion dollars on accessories such as hair product, make-up, cologne, and lotions. It's amazing to me that while we could not live without our extras—people were losing their jobs. Why? Because people are horrible at determining worth.

PEOPLE ARE HORRIBLE AT DETERMINIG WORTH

I have counseled, prayed for, and even helped countless students who have determined that they were worthless due to what somebody said, didn't say, or did to them. Friends stabbed them in the back, told their secrets, betrayed them—the list goes on and on. We spend our entire lives trying to please people who will probably change their minds on what is or is not worth something tomorrow.

I remember getting my first iPhone. I got the 3GS right after the 4 came out. I was super pumped about having an iPhone, yet when around all my friends who had the 4, it seemed like my 3GS was useless and unproductive. Right away, I started lusting for the iPhone 4—even though I just spent $200 canceling my previous contract with another provider and another $150 on the phone. My $350 investment seemed worthless because of what my friends were saying about the 4. Why does it seem like "worth" is always changing, like a moving target?

We must realize that humans are born with feelings. And those feelings can become so strong that they will make you believe they're true…even if they are a lie. Think about it—how many people do you know who think they are "fat" but are anything but that? How many people believe they are not "good looking," but you only wish you could be half as good looking as they are? Or how many people believe their parents are "poor" or "broke" just because they don't wear new clothes from the top brands—even though they may have a car, good clothes and a room full of cool things that really "broke" parents cannot buy?

Obviously, we need to find out what worth is. And it would probably be smart to go to someone who knows something about it.

WORTH IS FOUND IN WHAT SOMEONE IS WILLING TO PAY

I remember struggling with the problem of worth as a teenager. My whole worth was determined on if I made the team, had the right friends, and did the right things. The problem was that the things my friends wanted me to do to be cool—or worth something in their eyes—were the very things I knew were wrong. I knew what the Bible had said and even understood God's love. Yet I chose to allow what others thought or said to determine my worth more than what God did.

You would think this problem would go away once I got out of school. It didn't. It followed me to work, in my marriage, and everywhere else I went. I realized the problem was in me. I had a mind that was trained to live how I felt. But through the Bible and meditating on Scriptures, I found out that feelings are tricky little guys. My feelings had been trained to find worth based on what others said or did. As I began to realize how humans change their minds almost daily, I realized that I was looking for value in the wrong ways and from the wrong sources.

I'll never forget the day when the most common Scripture among Christians went from being common to a conviction. John 3:16 says, "For

God so loved the world, that he gave his one and only son, that whosoever believes in him, should not perish but have everlasting life."

When I really got this, I realized that He didn't die for just good people, He died for the world, which was full of bad people. Romans 5:7-8 says, "But God demonstrates his own love for us in this: While we were still sinners, Christ died for us."

God is the creator of the universe and the One before whom we will stand and give an account. And your friends, clothes, and accolades will amount to nothing.

But the One who knows all our ways, thoughts, and words says, "You are WORTH dying for!"

WOW! Imagine what your life would look like if you could look yourself in the mirror knowing that you are worth dying for. If you really believed that, imagine how other people's statements and actions would no longer keep you from trying what you've always wanted to try.

Imagine waking up in the morning and—regardless of the brand of clothing you wear, the style of your hair, or your weight—knowing that you are WORTH dying for.

Every girl's dream is to have a man who thinks she's worth dying for. Every guy wants a girl who thinks he's worth more than every other guy on the planet put together. God created all of us with the ability to feel worth something. He created us that way so that we can look at Him and truly receive His words, "YOU ARE WORTH DYING FOR!"

So what do we do with the feelings of worthlessness that come when the people we love the most reject us? How do we face rejection and a world full of people who are horrible at determining worth? And where do we go when it seems like what they are saying is true, worthless?

Glad you asked! Keep reading.

PART TWO:

STOP THINK AND LISTEN

If our lives are going to be productive, we are going to have to move our focus from people who are horrible at determining worth to "THE ONE" who determines the worth of all things. We can no longer allow others' words and actions to have the final word when it comes to our worth.

Sound simple? Well, it is definitely a challenge, but it has and can done—yes, even by you.

There was this guy who wasn't good at much. Well he was decent at one thing—hiding. The family this guy grew up in was not the toughest or the richest of families. Actually, quite the opposite. His dad was from the side of the family that never seemed to have the wealth, strength, or popularity that all the other uncles, aunts, and cousins had.

One day, as this guy is hiding from his family and enemies, one of the strangest things takes place. An angel appears! The angel comes and has the audacity to have a conversation with this lowly guy who is only good at hiding. "You mighty warrior! You are going to be the captain of the army of your family and deliver your family from years of slavery and hiding."

You would think this guy from humble beginnings would jump up and begin running in circles and telling all his cousins and brothers who'd picked on him his whole life what the angel said. But instead, the guy replies, "What? I am no captain. Actually, my family is a bunch of deadbeats, and I am the least of all of them. I think you have the wrong guy!"

Yet again, the angel repeats, "You mighty warrior! You are going to be the captain of the army of your family and deliver your family from years of slavery and hiding."

It takes a few minutes for it all to sink in, but finally the guy understands that this angel is a messenger from God. After finally realizing God is trying to say something, the guy finally puts away all the anger and the hurt from what his family, friends, and foes have said about him.

Finally, it sinks in.

This is the story of Gideon, who became one of the mightiest warriors in Israel's history. The Bible records in Judges 7, that Gideon took three hundred trumpet players and defeated thousands. He did so because he chose to believe what God said and not what anyone else had to say. He soon realized that God's words are so much more meaningful and powerful than those of others. Yet, he had to take the time to STOP, THINK, and LISTEN to what God had to say and dismiss what everyone else had said.

STOP, THINK, AND LISTEN is a process that I like to use when facing situations that seem impossible. Now "impossible" doesn't only mean things no one else has tried before. Impossible is anything that anyone—including yourself—has said you can't do. Too many times, things became impossible because we allowed what we or others have said to replace what God has said. We need to take a moment and just STOP all those thoughts of "I can't," "You'll never," "No one else has," or "They said I'm not."

Now you might argue that you cannot stop those kinds of thoughts. And the truth is you cannot stop them from popping into your mind—and that's basically what happens, isn't it? They just pop up. However, you can change them once they enter into your mind.

It's like when you are in the middle of the perfect dream. Maybe you're living the life you have always dreamed of, and the sound of your alarm wakes you up. The thoughts "Go back to sleep and finish this amazing dream," or "Just tell them you're sick so you can stay in bed all day" enter your mind. They seem so true and so right. Yet, you stop and think. If you're tardy to class once more, you will have to retake American History—and the first time was bad enough. So you make yourself get up, get ready, and get out the door.

The Bible says in Romans 12:2, "Do not be conformed to this world, but be transformed by the renewing of your mind."

The same way that a Transformer goes from being a sports car restricted to the highway to a fierce robot that destroys buildings and any other thing in its way, we too can be transformed through thinking something different. God has programmed us to be able to go from a nobody to a somebody—just by changing the way we think.

TAKE THE TİME

If you have a favorite movie, chances are you have watched it numerous times. You have probably watched it so often you can almost quote the entire movie. And right when the movie gets to the perfect scene, you close your eyes or turn to your friends and act out the part you have watched entirely too many times. The reason you were able to recite it from memory is that you have rehearsed it repeatedly—not only watching it on the screen but rewatching it in your mind over and over again. When you watch it take place in your mind, you are listening to it.

Romans 10:17 says, "Faith comes by hearing and hearing the message of Christ." Faith, or a conviction or belief, comes through hearing something over and over again. When we hear everyone else telling us we are worthless and pointless and that we cannot do this or that, it begins to create a "faith," a conviction or belief, in what we hear.

When thoughts of negativity, hate, anger, or worthlessness try to pop up in our mind, we need to STOP and then begin to THINK of what God says. Because when we begin to THINK on what God said in His Word that we "can do all things through Christ who gives me strength," or "with God, all things are possible," or "greater is He that is in me than he that is in the world," or "faith is the victory that overcomes the world," or "life nor death, nor angels or demons can separate me from the love of God. In all these things we are more than conquers through Christ Jesus our Lord" we will begin to LISTEN and hear how you can do and be everything others said you could not be.

I have personally found that when others say things that make me feel somewhat worthless, speaking God's Word out loud is one of the best ways to change what I'm thinking.

One day, after taking a new job, I made a horrible mistake. The guys who had worked there longer were coming down on me and making jokes about me. If there was a time I felt worthless, it was then. I went and looked myself in the mirror and pointed and said, "You are worth dying for!" Then I said it again, "YOU ARE WORTH DYING FOR!" I did so until the thoughts of what they had said disappeared and the only thing I was concentrating on was "I AM WORTH DYING FOR!"

THE WORK IS WORTH IT

David was just a "ruddy young lad" who was least among his brothers. His dad sent him to check up on his older brothers who got to go fight in a war (which was like being old enough to drive back in the day), and he found the entire army of Israel hiding from a giant named Goliath. David found his brothers and countrymen and tried to figure out what was going on.

The moment David found out the king would give great wealth, his daughter, and a tax free life, his older (obviously stronger, I might add) brother says, "Why have you come down here? And with whom did you leave those few sheep in the desert? I know how conceited you are and how wicked your heart is; you came down only to watch the battle."

Why did his brother say such a thing? Because David, this young boy among men said, "Who is this uncircumcised Philistine that he should defy the armies of the living God?" As we would say in my neighborhood, "Them's fighting words!" David knew what God's promise to Israel was. David had spent time listening to God's words. The promise that "no nation will be able to stand against you" was a sure thing in David's mind.

David could have listened to his brother, who obviously was lacking in the brotherly love, and had probably been picking on him his entire life. David could have ran back home to tell his dad how his older brothers never let him join in the fun or only viewed him as a tag along. Yet, because David took time to STOP, THINK, and LISTEN, he went another route.

The Bible records in 1 Samuel 17:30 that "He turned away [from his brother and other haters] to someone else and brought up the same matter..."

David chose not to allow his brothers words to stop him from doing something. David then found himself speaking to the king , guaranteeing victory, "Let no one lose heart on account of this Philistine; your servant will go and fight him." If you're not familiar with the rest of the story, this boy, who knew what God had said about Israel's enemies, went out and defeated

Goliath. This led to the whole army of Israel rising up and routing the Philistines. All because David chose to STOP, THINK, and LISTEN.

You must realize that it doesn't matter what anyone has said, done, or hasn't done—you are worth dying for. But if you are going to overcome the emotions and feelings of rejection and hurt, you will have to STOP, THINK, and LISTEN to what God has to say about you. It will take time and effort, but I will promise you this: If you take time to hear what God says about you, you will defeat many Goliaths in your lifetime.

Take time to review the following things that God says about you when you are facing situations that try to keep you from achieving your dreams. Take time and memorize and read them out loud, especially when what other people say create thoughts that are contrary.

Soon enough, like David, you'll be overcoming impossible situations, because you know your worth.

WHEN NEEDING COMFORT

2 CORINTHIANS 1:3-4 NIV

Praise be to the God and Father of our Lord Jesus Christ, the Father of compassion and the God of all comfort, who comforts us in all our troubles, so that we can comfort those in any trouble with the comfort we ourselves have received from God.

JOHN 14:16-17 KJV

And I will pray the Father, and he shall give you another Comforter, that he may abide with you for ever; even the Spirit of truth; whom the world cannot receive, because it seeith him not, neither knoweth him. but ye know him; for he dwelleth with you and shall be in you.

ISAIAH 61:1 NIV (EMPHASIS MINE)

The Spirit of the Sovereign Lord is on me, because the Lord has anointed me to proclaim good news to the poor. He has sent me to bind up *[like a book falling apart gets a new binding]* the brokenhearted.

WHEN NEEDING
DIRECTION

JOHN 14:26 NIV (EMPHASIS MINE)

But the Counselor, the Holy Spirit, whom the Father will send in my name, will teach you all things *[God's will for your life]* and will remind you of everything I have said to you.

1 CORINTHIANS 2:9-10 NIV (EMPHASIS MINE)

However, as it is written: "No eye has seen, no ear has heard, no mind has conceived what God has prepared for those who love him"—but God has revealed it to us by his Spirit. The Spirit searches all things, even the deep things of God *[things too deep for you to know or understand]*.

PROVERBS 3:5-6 NIV (EMPHASIS MINE)

Trust in the Lord with all your heart and lean not on your own understanding; in all your ways acknowledge him *[lean on God and let Him be your crutch, put all your weight on His ways]* and he will make your paths straight.

JAMES 1:5-6 NIV (EMPHASIS MINE)

If any of you lacks wisdom, he should ask God, who gives gen-erously to all without finding fault *[even if you got yourself in the mess],* and it will be given to him. But when he asks, he must believe and not doubt, because he who doubts is like a wave of the sea, blown and tossed by the wind.

COLOSSIANS 1:9 NIV (EMPHASIS MINE)

For this reason, since the day we heard about you, we have not stopped praying for you and asking God to fill you with the knowledge of his will through *all spiritual wisdom and understanding.*

WHEN NEEDING STRENGTH

PSALM 27:2-3 NIV

When evil men advance against me to devour my flesh, when my enemies and my foes attack me, they will stumble and fall. Though an army besiege me, my heart will not fear; though war break out against me, even then will I be confident.

PHILLIPIANS 4:12-13 AMP

I know how to abased and live humbly in straitened circumstances, and I know also how to enjoy plenty and live in abundance. I have learned in any and all circumstances the secret of facing every situation, whether well-fed or going hungry, having a sufficiency and enough or going without and being in want. I have strength for all things in Christ Who empowers me *[I am ready for anything and equal to anything through Him Who infuses inner strength into me; I am self-sufficient in Christ's sufficiency].*

EPHESIANS 6:10 AMP

In conclusion, be strong in the Lord [be empowered through your union with Him]; draw your strength from Him *[that strength which His boundless might provides].*

WHEN FACING IMPOSSIBLE SITUATIONS

ROMANS 8:28 NIV

And we know that in all things God works for the good of those who love him, who have been called according to his purpose.

ROMANS 8:31 NIV (EMPHASIS MINE)

What, then, shall we say in response to this? [*YOU HAVE TO SAY*] If God is for us, who can be against us?

EPHESIANS 6:12-13 AMP (EMPHASIS MINE)

For we are not wrestling with flesh and blood [contending only with the physical opponents], but against the despotisms, against the powers, against [the master spirits who are] the world rulers of this present darkness, against the forces of wickedness in heavenly (supernatural) sphere. Therefore put on Gods' complete armor, that you may be able to resist and stand your ground on the evil day [*of danger*], and, having done all [*the crisis demands*], to stand [*firmly in your place*].

JAMES 1:2-3 NIV (EMPHASIS MINE)

Consider [strongly think about] it pure joy, my brothers, whenever you face trials of many kinds, because you know that the testing of your faith develops perseverance (*the ability to stand longer and stronger*).

MATTHEW 19:26 NIV (EMPHASIS MINE)

But Jesus looked at them and said, "With men this is impossible, but all things are possible with [*through His ways*] God."

Also Available:

In *The Missing LİNK*, Jon Coats teaches you how to plug into the Source that will help you span the distance between what you want your life to be like and where it is through the power of the Holy Spirit.

When you empower your life with *The Missing LİNK*, you will discover the true nature of the believer and take the first steps of living a life remodeled to be like our ultimate example, Jesus Christ.